F

U.S. Department
of Transportation

**Federal Aviation
Administration**

Aviation Mechanic
General, Airframe, and Powerplant
Airman Certification Standards

November 1, 2021

* The Administrator of the Federal Aviation Administration signed the interim final rule "Part 147, Aviation Maintenance Technician Schools" on March 9, 2022. The interim final rule incorporates this version of the Aviation Mechanic General, Airframe, and Powerplant Airman Certification Standards (FAA-S-ACS-1) by reference. For identification and document-control purposes, this ACS is dated November 1, 2021. However, this ACS is not enforceable until the effective date of the interim final rule. Upon publication, the interim final rule can be found on the Federal Register's website, www.federalregister.gov, and will direct the effective date of compliance with this ACS.

**Flight Standards Service
Washington, DC 20591**

Foreword

The U.S. Department of Transportation (DOT), Federal Aviation Administration (FAA), Office of Safety Standards, Regulatory Support Division, Airman Testing Standards Branch has published the Aviation Mechanic General, Airframe, and Powerplant Airman Certification Standards (ACS) to communicate the aeronautical knowledge, risk management, and proficiency standards for the Mechanic Certificate.

Please send comments regarding this document using the following link to the Airman Testing Branch Mailbox.

Revision History

Document	Description	Revision Date
FAA-S-ACS-1	Aviation Mechanic - General, Airframe, and Powerplant Airman Certification Standards	11/01/2021

Table of Contents

I. General

Subject A. Fundamentals of Electricity and Electronics

Objective	*The following knowledge, risk management, and skill elements are required for basic electricity and electronics.*
Knowledge	*The applicant demonstrates understanding of:*
AM.I.A.K1	Electron theory (conventional flow vs. electron flow).
AM.I.A.K2	Magnetism.
AM.I.A.K3	Capacitance in a circuit.
AM.I.A.K4	Inductance in a circuit.
AM.I.A.K5	Alternating current (AC) electrical circuits.
AM.I.A.K6	Direct current (DC) electrical circuits.
AM.I.A.K7	Electrical laws and theory.
AM.I.A.K7a	a. Ohm's Law
AM.I.A.K7b	b. Kirchhoff's Laws
AM.I.A.K7c	c. Watt's Law
AM.I.A.K7d	d. Faraday's Law
AM.I.A.K7e	e. Lenz's Law
AM.I.A.K7f	f. Right-hand motor rule
AM.I.A.K8	Electrical measurement tools, principles, and procedures.
AM.I.A.K9	Voltage.
AM.I.A.K9a	a. Regulation
AM.I.A.K10	Current.
AM.I.A.K11	Resistance.
AM.I.A.K11a	a. Impedance
AM.I.A.K11b	b. Resistance in series
AM.I.A.K11c	c. Resistance in parallel
AM.I.A.K11d	d. Total resistance
AM.I.A.K12	Power.
AM.I.A.K13	Series circuits.
AM.I.A.K14	Parallel circuits.
AM.I.A.K15	Aircraft batteries.
AM.I.A.K16	Transformers.
AM.I.A.K17	Circuit continuity.
AM.I.A.K18	Controlling devices, including switches and relays.
AM.I.A.K19	Protective devices, including fuses, circuit breakers, and current limiters.
AM.I.A.K20	Resistor types and color coding.
AM.I.A.K21	Semiconductors, including diodes, transistors, and integrated circuits.

AM.I.A.K22	Digital logic, including RAM, ROM, NVRAM, logic gates, inverter, rectifier, and flip flop.
AM.I.A.K23	Binary numbers.
AM.I.A.K24	Electrostatic discharge.
AM.I.A.K25	Electrical circuit drawings.
AM.I.A.K26	Complex/combined circuits.
AM.I.A.K27	AC and DC motors.

Risk Management *The applicant demonstrates the ability to identify, assess, and mitigate risks associated with:*

AM.I.A.R1	Taking voltage, current, resistance, and capacitance measurements.
AM.I.A.R2	Handling, storage, and inspection of different types of batteries (i.e., lead acid, NiCad, lithium ion, gel cell).
AM.I.A.R3	High-voltage circuits (e.g., strobe lighting).
AM.I.A.R4	Working around batteries.

Skills *The applicant demonstrates the ability to:*

AM.I.A.S1	Perform circuit continuity test.
AM.I.A.S2	Measure voltage.
AM.I.A.S3	Measure current.
AM.I.A.S4	Measure resistance.
AM.I.A.S5	Test a switch or relay.
AM.I.A.S6	Test a fuse or circuit breaker.
AM.I.A.S7	Read and interpret aircraft electrical circuit diagrams, and symbols, including solid state devices and logic functions.
AM.I.A.S8	Troubleshoot a circuit.
AM.I.A.S9	Identify symbols used in electrical and electronic schematic diagrams (e.g., grounds, shields, resistors, capacitors, fuses, circuit breakers, batteries, diodes, transistors, and integrated circuits).
AM.I.A.S10	Demonstrate how to test for short-circuit and open-circuit conditions.
AM.I.A.S11	Measure voltage drop across a resistor.
AM.I.A.S12	Determine or measure for open electrical circuits.
AM.I.A.S13	Inspect an aircraft battery.
AM.I.A.S14	Service an aircraft battery.

I. General

Subject B. Aircraft Drawings

Objective	*The following knowledge, risk management, and skill elements are required for aircraft drawings.*
Knowledge	*The applicant demonstrates understanding of:*
AM.I.B.K1	Drawings, blueprints, sketches, charts, graphs, and system schematics, including commonly used lines, symbols, and terminology.
AM.I.B.K2	Repair or alteration of an aircraft system or component(s) using drawings, blueprints, or system schematics to determine whether it conforms to its type design.
AM.I.B.K3	Inspection of an aircraft system or component(s) using drawings, blueprints, or system schematics.
AM.I.B.K4	Terms used in conjunction with aircraft drawings, blueprints, or system schematics.
Risk Management	*The applicant demonstrates the ability to identify, assess, and mitigate risks associated with:*
AM.I.B.R1	Interpretation of plus or minus tolerances as depicted on aircraft drawings.
AM.I.B.R2	Specifications for design of alterations and repairs.
AM.I.B.R3	Applicability of the drawing or schematic to the particular aircraft by model and serial number.
AM.I.B.R4	Identification of the current version and applicability of drawing being used.
Skills	*The applicant demonstrates the ability to:*
AM.I.B.S1	Draw a sketch of a repair or alteration.
AM.I.B.S2	Identify the meaning of lines and symbols used in an aircraft drawing.
AM.I.B.S3	Interpret dimensions used in an aircraft drawing.
AM.I.B.S4	Identify changes on an aircraft drawing.
AM.I.B.S5	Determine material requirements from an aircraft drawing.
AM.I.B.S6	Interpret graphs and charts.

I. General

Subject C. Weight and Balance

Objective	*The following knowledge, risk management, and skill elements are required for weight and balance.*
Knowledge	*The applicant demonstrates understanding of:*
AM.I.C.K1	Weight and balance terminology.
AM.I.C.K2	Purpose for weighing an aircraft.
AM.I.C.K3	Weighing procedures, including the general preparations for weighing, with emphasis on aircraft weighing area considerations.
AM.I.C.K4	Procedures for calculation of the following: arm, positive or negative moment, center of gravity (CG), or moment index.
AM.I.C.K5	Purpose and application of weight and CG limits.
AM.I.C.K6	Purpose of determining CG.
AM.I.C.K7	Adverse loading considerations and how to calculate if adverse loading causes an out-of-limit condition.
AM.I.C.K8	Determine proper empty weight configuration.
AM.I.C.K9	Proper ballast placement.
AM.I.C.K10	Jacking an aircraft.
Risk Management	*The applicant demonstrates the ability to identify, assess, and mitigate risks associated with:*
AM.I.C.R1	Situations and conditions when jacking an aircraft.
AM.I.C.R2	Aircraft weighing procedures.
AM.I.C.R3	Use of scales.
AM.I.C.R4	Aerodynamic effect of CG that is forward or aft of CG limits.
AM.I.C.R5	Aerodynamic and performance effects of weight in excess of limits.
Skills	*The applicant demonstrates the ability to:*
AM.I.C.S1	Research and explain the procedures for weighing an aircraft.
AM.I.C.S2	Perform weight and balance calculations.
AM.I.C.S3	Calculate ballast weight shift and required weight location.
AM.I.C.S4	Check aircraft weighing scales for calibration.
AM.I.C.S5	Calculate weight and balance for an aircraft after an equipment change.
AM.I.C.S6	Compute forward and aft loaded CG limit.
AM.I.C.S7	Create a maintenance record for a weight and balance change.
AM.I.C.S8	Compute the empty weight and empty weight CG of an aircraft.
AM.I.C.S9	Calculate the moment of an item of equipment.
AM.I.C.S10	Identify tare items.
AM.I.C.S11	Locate weight and balance information.
AM.I.C.S12	Locate datum.
AM.I.C.S13	Locate weight and balance placarding and limitation requirements for an aircraft.
AM.I.C.S14	Revise an aircraft equipment list after equipment change.
AM.I.C.S15	Calculate the change needed to correct an out of balance condition.

AM.I.C.S16   Determine an aircraft's CG range using aircraft specifications, Type Certificate Data Sheets (TCDSs), and aircraft listings.

AM.I.C.S17   Calculate a weight change and complete required records.

I. General

Subject D. Fluid Lines and Fittings

Objective	*The following knowledge, risk management, and skill elements are required for fluid lines and fittings.*
Knowledge	*The applicant demonstrates understanding of:*
AM.I.D.K1	Tubing and hose materials, applications, sizes, and fittings.
AM.I.D.K2	Rigid line or flexible hose material identification.
AM.I.D.K3	Rigid line fabrication, installation, and inspection techniques/practices.
AM.I.D.K4	Flexible hose fabrication, installation, and inspection techniques/practices.
AM.I.D.K5	Importance of using a torque wrench when securing fluid hose and line fittings.
AM.I.D.K6	Use of torque seal or similar witness techniques after installing critical fluid hose and line fittings.
Risk Management	*The applicant demonstrates the ability to identify, assess, and mitigate risks associated with:*
AM.I.D.R1	System configuration prior to and during maintenance.
AM.I.D.R2	Use of required safety equipment.
AM.I.D.R3	Hazardous fluids.
AM.I.D.R4	High-pressure fluid systems.
AM.I.D.R5	A twisted hose.
AM.I.D.R6	A loosened fitting or a hose that has moved out of position.
AM.I.D.R7	Use of tools while applying torque to a fluid line.
Skills	*The applicant demonstrates the ability to:*
AM.I.D.S1	Fabricate a rigid line with a flare and a bend.
AM.I.D.S2	Install an aircraft rigid line.
AM.I.D.S3	Install an aircraft flexible hose.
AM.I.D.S4	Perform a rigid line or flexible hose inspection.
AM.I.D.S5	Identify installation and security requirements for rigid lines and flexible hoses.
AM.I.D.S6	Identify fluid lines, pneumatic lines, and fittings.
AM.I.D.S7	Fabricate a flexible hose.
AM.I.D.S8	Fabricate a flareless-fitting-tube connection.

I. General

Subject E. Aircraft Materials, Hardware, and Processes

Objective	The following knowledge, risk management, and skill elements are required for materials, hardware, and processes.

Knowledge — The applicant demonstrates understanding of:

AM.I.E.K1	Materials commonly used in aircraft and their general application.
AM.I.E.K2	Heat treatment and metal working processes.
AM.I.E.K3	Forces placed on aircraft materials (e.g., tension, compression, torsion, bending, strain, and shear).
AM.I.E.K4	Hardware commonly used in aircraft (e.g., bolts, nuts, screws, pins, washers, turnlock fasteners, cables, cable fittings, and rigid line couplings).
AM.I.E.K5	Safety wire and safety clip requirements and techniques.
AM.I.E.K6	Precision measurement tools, principles, and procedures.
AM.I.E.K7	Soldering preparation, types of solder, and flux usage.
AM.I.E.K8	Torquing tools, principles, and procedures.
AM.I.E.K9	Suitability and compatibility of materials and hardware used for maintenance.
AM.I.E.K10	Relationship between torque and fastener preload.
AM.I.E.K11	Identification markings on materials and hardware.
AM.I.E.K12	Characteristics of acceptable welds.
AM.I.E.K13	Characteristics of unacceptable welds.
AM.I.E.K14	Procedures for weld repairs.

Risk Management — The applicant demonstrates the ability to identify, assess, and mitigate risks associated with:

AM.I.E.R1	Use of personal protective equipment (PPE).
AM.I.E.R2	Improper torque.
AM.I.E.R3	Used hardware or suspected unapproved parts (SUPS).
AM.I.E.R4	Torquing techniques on critical, highly-stressed fasteners.

Skills — The applicant demonstrates the ability to:

AM.I.E.S1	Install safety wire on nuts, bolts, and turnbuckles.
AM.I.E.S2	Determine and properly torque aircraft hardware.
AM.I.E.S3	Inspect and check welds.
AM.I.E.S4	Identify aircraft materials and hardware based on manufacturer's markings.
AM.I.E.S5	Select and install aircraft bolts.
AM.I.E.S6	Make precision measurements with an instrument that has a Vernier scale.
AM.I.E.S7	Check the concentricity of a shaft.
AM.I.E.S8	Identify aircraft control cable components.
AM.I.E.S9	Fabricate a cable assembly using a swaged-end fitting.
AM.I.E.S10	Select the correct aluminum alloy for a structural repair.
AM.I.E.S11	Identify rivets by physical characteristics.
AM.I.E.S12	Determine suitability of materials for aircraft repairs.

| AM.I.E.S13 | Distinguish between heat-treated and non-heat-treated aluminum alloys. |
| AM.I.E.S14 | Check for proper calibration of a micrometer. |

I. General

Subject F. Ground Operations and Servicing

Objective		The following knowledge, risk management, and skill elements are required for ground operations and servicing.
Knowledge		The applicant demonstrates understanding of:
	AM.I.F.K1	Aircraft towing procedures.
	AM.I.F.K2	Aircraft securing procedures.
	AM.I.F.K3	Aviation fueling/defueling procedures.
	AM.I.F.K4	Airport operation area procedures and ATC communications, including runway incursion prevention.
	AM.I.F.K5	Engine starting, ground operation, and aircraft taxiing procedures.
	AM.I.F.K6	Types/classes of fire extinguishers and procedures.
	AM.I.F.K7	Aircraft oil, hydraulic and pneumatic, and deicing servicing procedures.
	AM.I.F.K8	Oxygen system servicing procedures.
	AM.I.F.K9	Characteristics of aviation gasoline and turbine fuels, including basic types and means of identification.
	AM.I.F.K10	Fuel additives commonly used in the field.
	AM.I.F.K11	Use of approved grades/types of fuel in aircraft engines.
	AM.I.F.K12	Tool and hardware use and accountability.
	AM.I.F.K13	Material handling.
	AM.I.F.K14	Parts protections.
	AM.I.F.K15	Hazardous materials, Safety Data Sheets (SDS), and PPE.
	AM.I.F.K16	Foreign object damage effects.
Risk Management		The applicant demonstrates the ability to identify, assess, and mitigate risks associated with:
	AM.I.F.R1	Preparing to tow an aircraft.
	AM.I.F.R2	Connecting external power equipment to an aircraft.
	AM.I.F.R3	Fueling/defueling ungrounded aircraft or using improper equipment.
	AM.I.F.R4	Misfueling and using incorrect or contaminated fuel.
	AM.I.F.R5	Oxygen system servicing.
	AM.I.F.R6	Engine start/run-up without using a checklist.
	AM.I.F.R7	Engine starting and ground operations.
	AM.I.F.R8	Engine starting and operation while troubleshooting or adjusting engine controls.
	AM.I.F.R9	Ground operation of an aircraft engine with cowling removed contrary to manufacturer instructions.
	AM.I.F.R10	Ground operation of aircraft in the vicinity of other aircraft or ground support equipment.
Skills		The applicant demonstrates the ability to:
	AM.I.F.S1	Perform a foreign object damage control procedure.
	AM.I.F.S2	Connect external power to an aircraft.
	AM.I.F.S3	Prepare an aircraft for towing.
	AM.I.F.S4	Use appropriate hand signals for the movement of aircraft.

AM.I.F.S5	Inspect an aircraft fuel system for water and foreign object debris (FOD) contamination.
AM.I.F.S6	Identify different grades of aviation fuel.
AM.I.F.S7	Select an approved fuel for an aircraft.
AM.I.F.S8	Prepare an aircraft for fueling.
AM.I.F.S9	Follow a checklist to start up or shut down an aircraft reciprocating or turbine engine.
AM.I.F.S10	Identify procedures for extinguishing fires in an engine induction system.
AM.I.F.S11	Secure an aircraft.
AM.I.F.S12	Locate and explain procedures for securing a turbine-powered aircraft after engine shutdown.

I. General

Subject G. Cleaning and Corrosion Control

Objective	*The following knowledge, risk management, and skill elements are required for cleaning and corrosion control.*
Knowledge	*The applicant demonstrates understanding of:*
AM.I.G.K1	Aircraft cleaning procedures.
AM.I.G.K2	Corrosion theory and causation.
AM.I.G.K3	Types and effects of corrosion.
AM.I.G.K4	Corrosion-prone areas in aircraft.
AM.I.G.K5	Corrosion preventive maintenance procedures.
AM.I.G.K6	Corrosion identification and inspection.
AM.I.G.K7	Corrosion removal and treatment procedures.
AM.I.G.K8	Corrosion preventive compounds (CPC) (e.g., waxy sealants, thin-film dielectrics).
AM.I.G.K9	Selection of optimal CPC and frequency of treatment.
AM.I.G.K10	Use of high-pressure application equipment.
AM.I.G.K11	Improper use of cleaners on aluminum or composite materials.
AM.I.G.K12	Dissimilar metals causing accelerated corrosion and role of protective barriers to mitigate this risk.
AM.I.G.K13	Conversion coatings.
AM.I.G.K14	Materials used for protection of airframe structures.
AM.I.G.K15	Primer materials.
AM.I.G.K16	Topcoat materials.
AM.I.G.K17	Surface preparation for a desired finishing material.
AM.I.G.K18	Effects of ambient conditions on finishing materials.
AM.I.G.K19	Effects of improper surface preparation on finishing materials.
AM.I.G.K20	Regulatory requirements for replacing identification, registration markings, and placards.
AM.I.G.K21	Inspection of aircraft finishes.
AM.I.G.K22	Safety practices/precautions when using finishing materials (e.g., PPE, fire prevention).
AM.I.G.K23	Finishing materials application techniques and practices.
AM.I.G.K24	Control surface balance considerations after refinishing.
Risk Management	*The applicant demonstrates the ability to identify, assess, and mitigate risks associated with:*
AM.I.G.R1	Health concerns when using paints, solvents, finishing materials, and processes.
AM.I.G.R2	Ventilation.
AM.I.G.R3	Identification of materials and processes to be used for cleaning or corrosion treatment on a given part or structure to prevent further damage.
AM.I.G.R4	SDS PPE instructions for products during removal and treatment of corrosion.
AM.I.G.R5	Working with flammable chemicals.
AM.I.G.R6	Disposal of chemicals and waste materials.
AM.I.G.R7	Use of PPE when working with paints and solvents.

AM.I.G.R8	Application of finishing materials.
Skills	*The applicant demonstrates the ability to:*
AM.I.G.S1	Perform a portion of an aircraft corrosion inspection.
AM.I.G.S2	Identify, select, and use aircraft corrosion prevention/cleaning materials.
AM.I.G.S3	Apply corrosion prevention/coating materials.
AM.I.G.S4	Inspect finishes and identify defects.
AM.I.G.S5	Inspect an aircraft compartment for corrosion.
AM.I.G.S6	Identify procedures to clean and protect plastics.
AM.I.G.S7	Determine location and size requirements for aircraft registration numbers.
AM.I.G.S8	Prepare composite surface for painting.
AM.I.G.S9	Identify finishing materials and appropriate thinners.
AM.I.G.S10	Layout and mask a surface in preparation for painting.
AM.I.G.S11	Prepare metal surface for painting.
AM.I.G.S12	Determine what paint system can be used on a given aircraft.
AM.I.G.S13	Apply etch solution and conversion coating.
AM.I.G.S14	Identify types of protective finishes.

I. General

Subject H. Mathematics

Objective   The following knowledge, risk management, and skill elements are required for mathematics as it relates to aircraft maintenance.

Knowledge   The applicant demonstrates understanding of:

AM.I.H.K1	Areas of various geometrical shapes.
AM.I.H.K2	Volumes of various geometrical shapes.
AM.I.H.K3	Definitions, descriptions and use of geometrical terms, including but not limited to any of the following: *polygon*, *pi*, *diameter*, *radius*, and *hypotenuse*.
AM.I.H.K4	Ratio problems, including examples of where or how they may be used in relation to aircraft maintenance or system(s) operation.
AM.I.H.K5	Proportion and percentage problems, including examples of where or how they may be used in relation to aircraft maintenance or system(s) operation.
AM.I.H.K6	Algebraic operations, including examples of where or how they may be used in relation to aircraft maintenance.
AM.I.H.K7	Conditions or areas in which metric conversion may be necessary.
AM.I.H.K8	Scientific (exponential) notation, decimal notation, fractional notation, binary notation, and conversion between these various forms of numeric notation.
AM.I.H.K9	Rounding numbers.
AM.I.H.K10	Powers and special powers.
AM.I.H.K11	Measurement systems.
AM.I.H.K12	Use of positive and negative integers in mathematical operations.
AM.I.H.K13	Basic mathematic functions (addition, subtraction, multiplication, division).

Risk Management   The applicant demonstrates the ability to identify, assess, and mitigate risks associated with:

AM.I.H.R1	Precedence of operations when solving an algebraic equation.
AM.I.H.R2	Use of both positive and negative integers in mathematical operations.
AM.I.H.R3	Rounding off calculations.

Skills   The applicant demonstrates the ability to:

AM.I.H.S1	Determine the square root of given numbers.
AM.I.H.S2	Compute the volume of a cylinder.
AM.I.H.S3	Compute the area of a wing.
AM.I.H.S4	Calculate the volume of a shape, such as a baggage compartment or fuel tank.
AM.I.H.S5	Convert between fractional and decimal numbers.
AM.I.H.S6	Compare two numerical values using ratios.
AM.I.H.S7	Compute compression ratio.
AM.I.H.S8	Compute the torque value when converting from inch-pounds to foot-pounds or from foot-pounds to inch-pounds.

I. General

Subject I. Regulations, Maintenance Forms, Records, and Publications

Objective	The following knowledge, risk management, and skill elements are required for regulations, maintenance forms, records, and publications.

Knowledge — The applicant demonstrates understanding of:

AM.I.I.K1	Privileges and limitations of a mechanic certificate.
AM.I.I.K2	Recent experience requirements and how to re-establish once lost.
AM.I.I.K3	Maintenance record entry for approval for return to service after maintenance and alterations.
AM.I.I.K4	Maintenance record entry for approval for return to service after inspection.
AM.I.I.K5	The purpose and use of FAA forms (e.g., FAA Forms 337, 8010-4, 8100-2, 8130-3).
AM.I.I.K6	Maintenance terminology as defined in 14 CFR part 1 (e.g., time in service, maintenance, preventive maintenance, major alteration, major repair, minor alteration, minor repair).
AM.I.I.K7	Criteria and responsibility for determining whether a repair or alteration is major or minor.
AM.I.I.K8	The regulatory framework, including general subject matter of the parts of 14 CFR relevant to aircraft maintenance and mechanics.
AM.I.I.K9	Agency publications and guidance materials, including aircraft specifications, TCDSs, advisory circulars (AC), and airworthiness directives (AD).
AM.I.I.K10	Alternative Method of Compliance (AMOC) for an AD.
AM.I.I.K11	Manufacturer publications, including maintenance manuals, service bulletins, maintenance alerts, and master minimum equipment lists.
AM.I.I.K12	FAA databases and resources available, including TCDSs and supplemental type certificates.
AM.I.I.K13	Compliance requirements for manufacturer-specified methods, techniques, and practices.
AM.I.I.K14	Compliance requirements for manufacturer-specified maintenance and inspection intervals.
AM.I.I.K15	FAA-approved maintenance data, including maintenance manuals and other methods, techniques, and practices acceptable by the administrator.
AM.I.I.K16	Difference between approved data and acceptable data, and when each is required.
AM.I.I.K17	FAA-approved airworthiness limitations.
AM.I.I.K18	Alert, caution, and warning indications; and the basic definition of *warnings*, *cautions*, and *notes* that are used in maintenance and operating manuals.
AM.I.I.K19	Inoperative equipment.
AM.I.I.K20	Discrepancy records or placards.
AM.I.I.K21	Usable on (effectivity) codes in parts manuals.
AM.I.I.K22	Methods used to establish the serial number effectivity of an item.
AM.I.I.K23	Mechanic address change notification procedures.

Risk Management — The applicant demonstrates the ability to identify, assess, and mitigate risks associated with:

AM.I.I.R1	Completeness or accuracy of documentation.
AM.I.I.R2	Use of SDS.
AM.I.I.R3	Complacency during documentation phase of maintenance procedures.
AM.I.I.R4	Adherence to warnings, cautions, or notes in maintenance and operational manuals.
AM.I.I.R5	Determination of component applicability to a given aircraft.

Skills	*The applicant demonstrates the ability to:*
AM.I.I.S1	Complete an FAA Form 337 for a major repair or alteration.
AM.I.I.S2	Examine an FAA Form 337 for accuracy.
AM.I.I.S3	Determine an aircraft's inspection status by reviewing the aircraft's maintenance records.
AM.I.I.S4	Complete an aircraft maintenance record entry for the compliance of a reoccurring AD for a specific airframe, aircraft engine, appliance, or propeller.
AM.I.I.S5	Compare an equipment list for an aircraft to equipment installed.
AM.I.I.S6	Locate applicable FAA aircraft specifications and FAA TCDS for an aircraft or component.
AM.I.I.S7	Complete an aircraft maintenance record entry for return to service.
AM.I.I.S8	Determine applicability of an AD.
AM.I.I.S9	Check a Technical Standard Order (TSO) or part manufacturing authorization for the proper markings.
AM.I.I.S10	Use a manufacturer's illustrated parts catalog to locate a specific part number and applicability.
AM.I.I.S11	Locate supplemental type certificates applicable to a specific aircraft.
AM.I.I.S12	Determine the conformity of aircraft instrument range markings and placarding.
AM.I.I.S13	Determine approved replacement parts for installation on a given aircraft.
AM.I.I.S14	Determine maximum allowable weight of a specific aircraft.
AM.I.I.S15	Determine whether a given repair or alteration is major or minor.
AM.I.I.S16	Determine applicability of approved data for a major repair.
AM.I.I.S17	Explain the difference between "approved data" (required for major repair/alteration) and "acceptable data" (required for minor repair/alteration).
AM.I.I.S18	Complete a 100-hour inspection aircraft maintenance record entry.

I. General

Subject J. Physics for Aviation

Objective
The following knowledge, risk management, and skill elements are required for aviation physics.

Knowledge
The applicant demonstrates understanding of:

AM.I.J.K1	Matter and energy.
AM.I.J.K2	Work, power, force, and motion.
AM.I.J.K3	Simple machines and mechanics.
AM.I.J.K4	Heat and pressure.
AM.I.J.K5	Bernoulli's Principle.
AM.I.J.K6	Newton's Law of Motion.
AM.I.J.K7	Gas law and fluid mechanics.
AM.I.J.K8	Theory of flight (aerodynamics).
AM.I.J.K9	Standard atmosphere and factors affecting atmospheric conditions.
AM.I.J.K10	Primary and secondary aircraft flight controls.
AM.I.J.K11	Additional aerodynamic devices, including vortex generators, wing fences, and stall strips.
AM.I.J.K12	Relationship between temperature, density, weight, and volume.
AM.I.J.K13	Force, area, or pressure in a specific application.

Risk Management
The applicant demonstrates the ability to identify, assess, and mitigate risks associated with:

AM.I.J.R1	Changes in aircraft and engine performance due to density altitude.
AM.I.J.R2	Effect a repair can have on a flight surface.
AM.I.J.R3	Use of performance/testing data.
AM.I.J.R4	Use of related units of measure (e.g., Celsius vs. Fahrenheit).

Skills
The applicant demonstrates the ability to:

AM.I.J.S1	Convert temperature units (e.g., from Celsius to Fahrenheit).
AM.I.J.S2	Determine density altitude.
AM.I.J.S3	Determine pressure altitude.
AM.I.J.S4	Calculate force, area, or pressure in a specific application.
AM.I.J.S5	Demonstrate the mechanical advantage of various types of levers.
AM.I.J.S6	Design an inclined plane on paper, indicating the mechanical advantage.
AM.I.J.S7	Identify changes in pressure and velocity as a fluid passes through a venturi.
AM.I.J.S8	Calculate horsepower.

I. General

Subject K. Inspection Concepts and Techniques

Objective	*The following knowledge, risk management, and skill elements are required for aircraft inspection concepts and techniques.*
Knowledge	*The applicant demonstrates understanding of:*
AM.I.K.K1	Measuring tools, including calipers, micrometers, and gauges.
AM.I.K.K2	Calibration and tool accuracy requirements.
AM.I.K.K3	Nondestructive Testing (NDT) procedures and methods.
AM.I.K.K4	Aircraft inspection programs (e.g., progressive, 100-hour, annual, and other FAA-approved inspections).
AM.I.K.K5	Aircraft inspection methods and tools for materials, hardware, and processes.
Risk Management	*The applicant demonstrates the ability to identify, assess, and mitigate risks associated with:*
AM.I.K.R1	Demagnetizing a component following a magnetic particle inspection.
AM.I.K.R2	Using precision measuring instruments.
AM.I.K.R3	Calibration of precision measuring equipment.
AM.I.K.R4	Selection of inspection techniques.
AM.I.K.R5	Damage prevention to aircraft components and test equipment when using an ohmmeter.
Skills	*The applicant demonstrates the ability to:*
AM.I.K.S1	Use Vernier calipers.
AM.I.K.S2	Use micrometers.
AM.I.K.S3	Use measurement gauges.
AM.I.K.S4	Perform a visual inspection.
AM.I.K.S5	Perform a dye penetrant inspection.
AM.I.K.S6	Inspect aircraft for compliance with an AD.
AM.I.K.S7	Identify NDT methods for composite, surface metal, and subsurface metal defects.
AM.I.K.S8	Perform a tap test on a composite component.

I. General

Subject L. Human Factors

Objective		*The following knowledge, risk management, and skill elements are required for human factors.*
Knowledge		*The applicant demonstrates understanding of:*
	AM.I.L.K1	Safety culture and organizational factors.
	AM.I.L.K2	Human error principles.
	AM.I.L.K3	Event investigation.
	AM.I.L.K4	Human performance and limitations.
	AM.I.L.K5	Physical and social environment.
	AM.I.L.K6	Communication/reporting of hazards.
	AM.I.L.K7	Teamwork and leadership.
	AM.I.L.K8	Professionalism and integrity.
	AM.I.L.K9	Shift and task turnover.
	AM.I.L.K10	Conditions/preconditions for unsafe acts.
	AM.I.L.K11	Types of human errors.
Risk Management		*The applicant demonstrates the ability to identify, assess, and mitigate risks associated with:*
	AM.I.L.R1	Selective reporting of hazards.
	AM.I.L.R2	Fatigue management and fitness for duty.
	AM.I.L.R3	Non-invasive, condition-monitoring technologies.
Skills		*The applicant demonstrates the ability to:*
	AM.I.L.S1	File a Malfunction or Defect Report.
	AM.I.L.S2	Brief a shift turnover for continuity of work.
	AM.I.L.S3	Locate information regarding human factors errors.

II. Airframe

Subject A. Metallic Structures

Objective		*The following knowledge, risk management, and skill elements are required for aircraft metallic structures.*
Knowledge		*The applicant demonstrates understanding of:*
	AM.II.A.K1	Inspection/testing of metal structures.
	AM.II.A.K2	Types of sheet metal defects.
	AM.II.A.K3	Selection of sheet metal repair materials.
	AM.II.A.K4	Layout, forming, and drilling of sheet metal components.
	AM.II.A.K5	Selection of rivets, hardware, and fasteners for a sheet metal repair.
	AM.II.A.K6	Heat treatment processes for aluminum.
	AM.II.A.K7	Rivet layout.
	AM.II.A.K8	Rivet removal and installation methods.
	AM.II.A.K9	Maintenance safety practices/precautions for sheet metal repairs or fabrications.
	AM.II.A.K10	Flame welding gases.
	AM.II.A.K11	Storage/handling of welding gases.
	AM.II.A.K12	Flame welding practices and techniques.
	AM.II.A.K13	Inert-gas welding practices and techniques.
	AM.II.A.K14	Purpose and types of shielding gases.
	AM.II.A.K15	Types of steel tubing welding repairs.
	AM.II.A.K16	Procedures for weld repairs.
	AM.II.A.K17	Types of structures and their characteristics.
Risk Management		*The applicant demonstrates the ability to identify, assess, and mitigate risks associated with:*
	AM.II.A.R1	Selection of repair materials.
	AM.II.A.R2	Utilizing maintenance safety practices/precautions for sheet metal structures.
	AM.II.A.R3	Use of PPE when working with sheet metal structures.
	AM.II.A.R4	Handling, storage, and use of compressed gas bottles.
	AM.II.A.R5	Use of electric welding equipment.
Skills		*The applicant demonstrates the ability to:*
	AM.II.A.S1	Install and remove solid rivets.
	AM.II.A.S2	Install and remove a blind rivet.
	AM.II.A.S3	Determine applicability of sheet metal for a repair in a specific application.
	AM.II.A.S4	Select and install special purpose fasteners.
	AM.II.A.S5	Design a repair using a manufacturer's structural repair manual.
	AM.II.A.S6	Prepare and install a patch to repair an aircraft or component.
	AM.II.A.S7	Make a drawing of a repair, including the number of rivets and size of sheet metal required.
	AM.II.A.S8	Remove a repair that was installed with rivets.
	AM.II.A.S9	Trim and form a piece of sheet metal to fit a prepared area.

AM.II.A.S10	Fabricate an aluminum part in accordance with a drawing.
AM.II.A.S11	Determine a rivet pattern for a specific repair.
AM.II.A.S12	Countersink rivet holes in sheet metal.
AM.II.A.S13	Perform a repair on a damaged aluminum sheet.
AM.II.A.S14	Determine extent of damage and decide if metallic structure is repairable.

II. Airframe

Subject B. Non-Metallic Structures

Objective — The following knowledge, risk management, and skill elements are required for aircraft non-metallic structures.

Knowledge — The applicant demonstrates understanding of:

AM.II.B.K1	Wood structures, including inspection techniques, tools, and practices for wood structures.
AM.II.B.K2	Effects of moisture/humidity on wood and fabric coverings.
AM.II.B.K3	Types and general characteristics of wood used in aircraft structures.
AM.II.B.K4	Permissible substitutes and other materials used in the construction and repair of wood structures.
AM.II.B.K5	Acceptable and unacceptable wood defects.
AM.II.B.K6	Wood repair techniques and practices.
AM.II.B.K7	Factors used in determining the proper type covering material.
AM.II.B.K8	Types of approved aircraft covering material.
AM.II.B.K9	Seams commonly used with aircraft covering.
AM.II.B.K10	Covering textile terms.
AM.II.B.K11	Structure surface preparation.
AM.II.B.K12	Covering methods commonly used.
AM.II.B.K13	Covering means of attachment.
AM.II.B.K14	Areas on aircraft covering most susceptible to deterioration.
AM.II.B.K15	Aircraft covering preservation/restoration.
AM.II.B.K16	Inspection of aircraft covering.
AM.II.B.K17	Covering repair techniques and practices.
AM.II.B.K18	Inspection/testing of composite structures.
AM.II.B.K19	Types of composite structure defects.
AM.II.B.K20	Composite structure fiber, core, and matrix materials.
AM.II.B.K21	Composite materials storage practices and shelf life.
AM.II.B.K22	Composite repair methods, techniques, fasteners, and practices.
AM.II.B.K23	Thermoplastic material inspection/types of defects.
AM.II.B.K24	Thermoplastic material storage and handling.
AM.II.B.K25	Thermoplastic material installation procedures.
AM.II.B.K26	Care and maintenance of windows.
AM.II.B.K27	Window temporary and permanent repairs.
AM.II.B.K28	Maintenance safety practices/precautions for composite materials/structures, and windows.
AM.II.B.K29	Inspecting restraints and upholstery.

Risk Management — The applicant demonstrates the ability to identify, assess, and mitigate risks associated with:

AM.II.B.R1	Selection of glue (adhesive) or fasteners for aircraft structure.
AM.II.B.R2	Composite structure repairs.

AM.II.B.R3	Exposure to materials used in composite repair.
AM.II.B.R4	Storage of composite materials.
AM.II.B.R5	Measuring and mixing of materials associated with composite construction.
AM.II.B.R6	Use of materials that are not part of an approved repair system.
AM.II.B.R7	Material shelf-life.
Skills	*The applicant demonstrates the ability to:*
AM.II.B.S1	Identify appropriate fasteners on composite structures.
AM.II.B.S2	Inspect and repair fiberglass.
AM.II.B.S3	Inspect composite, plastic, or glass-laminated structures.
AM.II.B.S4	Clean and inspect acrylic type windshields.
AM.II.B.S5	Locate and explain procedures for a temporary repair to a side window.
AM.II.B.S6	Locate and explain the procedures for tying a modified seine knot.
AM.II.B.S7	Prepare composite surface for painting.
AM.II.B.S8	Perform a tap test on composite material.
AM.II.B.S9	Locate and explain repair standard dimensions.
AM.II.B.S10	Locate and explain repair procedures for elongated bolt holes.
AM.II.B.S11	Determine extent of damage and decide if nonmetallic structure is repairable.
AM.II.B.S12	Perform lay up for a repair to a composite panel, including preparation for vacuum bagging, using a manufacturer's repair manual.

II. Airframe

Subject C. Flight Controls

Objective	*The following knowledge, risk management, and skill elements are required for aircraft flight controls.*
Knowledge	*The applicant demonstrates understanding of:*

AM.II.C.K1	Control cables.
AM.II.C.K2	Control cable maintenance.
AM.II.C.K3	Cable connectors.
AM.II.C.K4	Cable guides.
AM.II.C.K5	Control stops.
AM.II.C.K6	Push-pull tubes.
AM.II.C.K7	Torque tubes.
AM.II.C.K8	Bellcranks.
AM.II.C.K9	Flutter and flight control balance.
AM.II.C.K10	Rigging of aircraft flight controls.
AM.II.C.K11	Aircraft flight controls and stabilizer systems.
AM.II.C.K12	Other aerodynamic wing features.
AM.II.C.K13	Secondary and auxiliary control surfaces.

Risk Management	*The applicant demonstrates the ability to identify, assess, and mitigate risks associated with:*

AM.II.C.R1	Use of and interpretation of a cable tension chart.
AM.II.C.R2	Rigging aircraft flight controls.
AM.II.C.R3	Selection and use of lifting equipment used to move aircraft components into place for assembly.
AM.II.C.R4	Maintaining a calibration schedule for cable tension meters and other rigging equipment.
AM.II.C.R5	Use and interpretation of cable tensiometers.

Skills	*The applicant demonstrates the ability to:*

AM.II.C.S1	Identify fixed-wing aircraft rigging adjustment locations.
AM.II.C.S2	Identify control surfaces that provide movement about an aircraft's axes.
AM.II.C.S3	Inspect a primary and secondary flight control surface.
AM.II.C.S4	Remove and reinstall a primary flight control surface.
AM.II.C.S5	Inspect primary control cables.
AM.II.C.S6	Adjust and secure a primary flight control cable.
AM.II.C.S7	Adjust push-pull flight control systems.
AM.II.C.S8	Check the balance of a flight control surface.
AM.II.C.S9	Determine allowable axial play limits for a flight control bearing.
AM.II.C.S10	Inspect a trim tab for freeplay, travel, and operation.
AM.II.C.S11	Balance a control surface.
AM.II.C.S12	Fabricate a primary flight control cable.

II. Airframe

Subject D. Airframe Inspection

Objective	*The following knowledge, risk management, and skill elements are required for airframe inspections.*
Knowledge	*The applicant demonstrates understanding of:*
AM.II.D.K1	Inspection requirements under 14 CFR part 91.
AM.II.D.K2	Maintenance recordkeeping requirements under 14 CFR part 43.
AM.II.D.K3	Requirements for complying with ADs.
AM.II.D.K4	Identification of life-limited parts and their replacement interval.
AM.II.D.K5	Special inspections.
AM.II.D.K6	Use of FAA-approved data.
AM.II.D.K7	Compliance with service letters, service bulletins, instructions for continued airworthiness, or ADs.
AM.II.D.K8	CFRs applicable to inspection and airworthiness.
AM.II.D.K9	Corrosion types and identification.
Risk Management	*The applicant demonstrates the ability to identify, assess, and mitigate risks associated with:*
AM.II.D.R1	Interpretation of inspection instructions, which can lead to over or under maintenance being performed.
AM.II.D.R2	Visual inspection and where to apply it.
AM.II.D.R3	Performing radiographic inspections.
AM.II.D.R4	Selection and use of checklists and other maintenance publications.
AM.II.D.R5	Maintenance record documentation.
Skills	*The applicant demonstrates the ability to:*
AM.II.D.S1	Perform an airframe inspection, including a records check.
AM.II.D.S2	Perform a portion of a 100-hour inspection in accordance with 14 CFR part 43.
AM.II.D.S3	Enter results of a 100-hour inspection in a maintenance record.
AM.II.D.S4	Determine compliance with a specific AD.
AM.II.D.S5	Provide a checklist for conducting a 100-hour inspection.
AM.II.D.S6	Determine if any additional inspections are required during a particular 100-hour inspection; (i.e., 300-hour filter replacement).
AM.II.D.S7	Inspect seat and seatbelt, including TSO markings.

II. Airframe

Subject E. Landing Gear Systems

Objective	*The following knowledge, risk management, and skill elements are required for aircraft landing gear systems.*
Knowledge	*The applicant demonstrates understanding of:*

AM.II.E.K1	Fixed and retractable landing gear systems.
AM.II.E.K2	Fixed and retractable landing gear components.
AM.II.E.K3	Landing gear strut servicing/lubrication.
AM.II.E.K4	Inspection of bungee and spring steel landing gear systems.
AM.II.E.K5	Steering systems.
AM.II.E.K6	Landing gear position and warning system inspection, check, and servicing.
AM.II.E.K7	Brake assembly servicing and inspection.
AM.II.E.K8	Anti-skid system components and operation.
AM.II.E.K9	Wheel, brake, and tire construction.
AM.II.E.K10	Tire storage, care, and servicing.
AM.II.E.K11	Landing gear and tire and wheel safety and inspection.
AM.II.E.K12	Brake actuating systems.
AM.II.E.K13	Alternative landing gear systems (e.g., skis, floats).

Risk Management	*The applicant demonstrates the ability to identify, assess, and mitigate risks associated with:*

AM.II.E.R1	Landing gear and tire and wheel practices/precautions.
AM.II.E.R2	Use of aircraft jacks.
AM.II.E.R3	High pressure fluids and gases.
AM.II.E.R4	Storage and handling of hydraulic fluids.
AM.II.E.R5	High pressure strut or system disassembly.
AM.II.E.R6	Operation of retractable landing gear systems around personnel.

Skills	*The applicant demonstrates the ability to:*

AM.II.E.S1	Inspect and service landing gear.
AM.II.E.S2	Inspect, check, and service an anti-skid system.
AM.II.E.S3	Locate and explain procedures for checking operation of an anti-skid warning system.
AM.II.E.S4	Locate and explain troubleshooting procedures for an anti-skid system.
AM.II.E.S5	Jack aircraft.
AM.II.E.S6	Troubleshoot a landing gear retraction check.
AM.II.E.S7	Inspect wheels, brakes, bearings, and tires.
AM.II.E.S8	Remove and replace brake lining(s).
AM.II.E.S9	Service landing gear air/oil shock strut.
AM.II.E.S10	Bleed air from a hydraulic brake system.
AM.II.E.S11	Troubleshoot hydraulic brake systems.
AM.II.E.S12	Remove, inspect, and install a wheel brake assembly.

AM.II.E.S13	Inspect a tire for defects.
AM.II.E.S14	Locate tire storage practices.
AM.II.E.S15	Replace air/oil shock strut air valve.
AM.II.E.S16	Troubleshoot an air/oil shock strut.
AM.II.E.S17	Service a nose-wheel shimmy damper.
AM.II.E.S18	Inspect nose-wheel steering system for proper adjustment.
AM.II.E.S19	Locate and explain the process for checking landing gear alignment.
AM.II.E.S20	Replace master brake cylinder packing seals.
AM.II.E.S21	Troubleshoot aircraft steering system.
AM.II.E.S22	Identify landing gear position and warning system components.
AM.II.E.S23	Troubleshoot landing gear position and warning systems.
AM.II.E.S24	Inspect and repair landing gear position indicating system.
AM.II.E.S25	Adjust the operation of a landing gear warning system.
AM.II.E.S26	Remove, install, and adjust a landing gear down-lock switch.
AM.II.E.S27	Inspect a brake for serviceability.
AM.II.E.S28	Troubleshoot nose-wheel shimmy.
AM.II.E.S29	Inspect tube landing gear for damage.

II. Airframe

Subject F. Hydraulic and Pneumatic Systems

Objective	*The following knowledge, risk management, and skill elements are required for aircraft hydraulic and pneumatic systems.*
Knowledge	*The applicant demonstrates understanding of:*
AM.II.F.K1	Hydraulic system components and fluids.
AM.II.F.K2	Hydraulic system operation.
AM.II.F.K3	Hydraulic system servicing requirements.
AM.II.F.K4	Hydraulic system inspection, check, servicing, and troubleshooting.
AM.II.F.K5	Pneumatic system types and components.
AM.II.F.K6	Pneumatic system servicing requirements.
AM.II.F.K7	Servicing, function, and operation of accumulators.
AM.II.F.K8	Types of hydraulic/pneumatic seals and fluid/seal compatibility.
AM.II.F.K9	Hoses, lines, and fittings.
AM.II.F.K10	Pressure regulators, restrictors, and valves.
AM.II.F.K11	Filter maintenance procedures.
Risk Management	*The applicant demonstrates the ability to identify, assess, and mitigate risks associated with:*
AM.II.F.R1	Relieving system pressure prior to system servicing or disassembly.
AM.II.F.R2	High pressure gases and fluids.
AM.II.F.R3	Storage and handling of hydraulic fluids.
AM.II.F.R4	Cross-contamination of hydraulic fluids.
AM.II.F.R5	Compatibility between hydraulic seals and hydraulic fluids.
Skills	*The applicant demonstrates the ability to:*
AM.II.F.S1	Identify different types of hydraulic fluids.
AM.II.F.S2	Identify different packing seals.
AM.II.F.S3	Install seals and backup rings in a hydraulic component.
AM.II.F.S4	Remove and install a selector valve.
AM.II.F.S5	Check a pressure regulator and adjust as necessary.
AM.II.F.S6	Remove, clean, inspect, and install a hydraulic system filter.
AM.II.F.S7	Service a hydraulic system accumulator.
AM.II.F.S8	Service a hydraulic system reservoir.
AM.II.F.S9	Remove, install, and perform an operational check of a hydraulic pump.
AM.II.F.S10	Locate procedures for checking pneumatic/bleed air overheat warning systems.
AM.II.F.S11	Purge air from a hydraulic system.
AM.II.F.S12	Remove and install a system pressure relief valve.
AM.II.F.S13	Inspect a hydraulic or pneumatic system for leaks.
AM.II.F.S14	Troubleshoot a hydraulic or pneumatic system for leaks.

AM.II.F.S15	Locate and explain hydraulic fluid servicing instructions and identify/select fluid for a given aircraft.
AM.II.F.S16	Locate installation procedures for a seal, backup ring, or gasket.

II. Airframe

Subject G. Environmental Systems

Objective	*The following knowledge, risk management, and skill elements are required for aircraft environmental systems.*
Knowledge	*The applicant demonstrates understanding of:*
AM.II.G.K1	Pressurization systems.
AM.II.G.K2	Bleed air heating.
AM.II.G.K3	Aircraft instrument cooling.
AM.II.G.K4	Exhaust heat exchanger and system component(s) function, operation, and inspection procedures.
AM.II.G.K5	Combustion heater and system component(s) function, operation, and inspection procedures.
AM.II.G.K6	Vapor-cycle system and system component(s) operation, servicing, and inspection procedures.
AM.II.G.K7	Air-cycle system and system component(s) operation and inspection procedures.
AM.II.G.K8	Cabin pressurization and system component(s) operation and inspection procedures.
AM.II.G.K9	Types of oxygen systems and oxygen system component(s) operation (e.g., chemical generator, pressure cylinder).
AM.II.G.K10	Oxygen system maintenance and inspection procedures.
Risk Management	*The applicant demonstrates the ability to identify, assess, and mitigate risks associated with:*
AM.II.G.R1	Oxygen system maintenance.
AM.II.G.R2	Recovery of vapor-cycle refrigerant.
AM.II.G.R3	Handling or performing maintenance on, chemical oxygen generating systems.
AM.II.G.R4	Storage, handling, and use of compressed gas cylinder and high pressure systems.
AM.II.G.R5	Manufacturer's recommended servicing procedures, including refrigerant types.
AM.II.G.R6	Maintenance of combustion heaters.
Skills	*The applicant demonstrates the ability to:*
AM.II.G.S1	Inspect an oxygen system.
AM.II.G.S2	Purge an oxygen system prior to servicing.
AM.II.G.S3	Service an oxygen system.
AM.II.G.S4	Clean and inspect a pilot emergency oxygen mask and supply hoses.
AM.II.G.S5	Inspect an oxygen system pressure regulator.
AM.II.G.S6	Inspect an oxygen system cylinder for serviceability.
AM.II.G.S7	Inspect a chemical oxygen generator for serviceability and safe handling.
AM.II.G.S8	Locate the procedures to troubleshoot a combustion heater.
AM.II.G.S9	Locate the procedures for servicing a refrigerant (vapor-cycle) system.
AM.II.G.S10	Inspect a combustion heater fuel system for leaks.
AM.II.G.S11	Locate the troubleshooting procedures for an air-cycle system.
AM.II.G.S12	Troubleshoot an air-cycle air conditioning system.
AM.II.G.S13	Inspect a cabin heater system equipped with an exhaust heat exchanger for cracks.
AM.II.G.S14	Clean and inspect an outflow valve for a pressurization system.

AM.II.G.S15   Locate troubleshooting procedures for a pressurization system.

31

II. Airframe

Subject H. Aircraft Instrument Systems

Objective	*The following knowledge, risk management, and skill elements are required for aircraft instrument systems.*
Knowledge	*The applicant demonstrates understanding of:*
AM.II.H.K1	Annunciator indicating systems and the meaning of warning, caution, and advisory lights.
AM.II.H.K2	Magnetic compass inspection and operation.
AM.II.H.K3	Magnetic compass swinging procedures.
AM.II.H.K4	Pressure indicating instruments.
AM.II.H.K5	Temperature indicating instruments.
AM.II.H.K6	Position indication sensors and instruments.
AM.II.H.K7	Gyroscopic instruments.
AM.II.H.K8	Direction indicating instruments.
AM.II.H.K9	Instrument vacuum and pneumatic systems.
AM.II.H.K10	Pitot-static system.
AM.II.H.K11	Fuel quantity indicating systems.
AM.II.H.K12	Instrument range markings.
AM.II.H.K13	Electronic displays.
AM.II.H.K14	Electrostatic sensitive devices.
AM.II.H.K15	Built-in test equipment.
AM.II.H.K16	Electronic flight instrument system.
AM.II.H.K17	Engine indication and crew alerting system.
AM.II.H.K18	Head-up displays (HUDs).
AM.II.H.K19	14 CFR parts 43 and 91 requirements for static system leak checks.
AM.II.H.K20	Instrument limitations, conditions, and characteristics.
AM.II.H.K21	Angle of attack and stall warning systems.
AM.II.H.K22	Takeoff and landing gear configuration warning systems.
AM.II.H.K23	Aircraft bonding and protection.
AM.II.H.K24	Instrument or instrument panel removal and installation.
Risk Management	*The applicant demonstrates the ability to identify, assess, and mitigate risks associated with:*
AM.II.H.R1	Use of pressurized air and water during maintenance or cleaning of aircraft instrument systems.
AM.II.H.R2	Actions in response to a reported intermittent warning or caution annunciator light illumination.
AM.II.H.R3	Performing maintenance on equipment identified as electrostatic-sensitive.
AM.II.H.R4	Handling of mechanical gyros or instruments containing mechanical gyros.
AM.II.H.R5	Performing a pitot/static system test.
Skills	*The applicant demonstrates the ability to:*
AM.II.H.S1	Perform a static system leak test.
AM.II.H.S2	Remove and install an instrument.

AM.II.H.S3	Install range marks on an instrument glass.
AM.II.H.S4	Determine barometric pressure using an altimeter.
AM.II.H.S5	Check for proper range markings on an instrument.
AM.II.H.S6	Inspect a magnetic compass.
AM.II.H.S7	Locate the procedures for troubleshooting a vacuum-operated instrument system.
AM.II.H.S8	Select proper altimeter for installation on a given aircraft.
AM.II.H.S9	Identify exhaust gas temperature system components.
AM.II.H.S10	Inspect a vacuum system filter for serviceability.
AM.II.H.S11	Adjust gyro/instrument air pressure/vacuum.
AM.II.H.S12	Inspect an aircraft's alternate air (static) source.
AM.II.H.S13	Locate and explain the adjustment procedures for a stall warning system.
AM.II.H.S14	Inspect outside air temperature gauge for condition and operation.

II. Airframe

Subject I. Communication and Navigation Systems

Objective	*The following knowledge, risk management, and skill elements are required for aircraft communication and navigation systems.*
Knowledge	*The applicant demonstrates understanding of:*
AM.II.I.K1	Radio operating principles.
AM.II.I.K2	Radio components.
AM.II.I.K3	Antenna, static discharge wicks, and avionics identification, inspection, and mounting requirements.
AM.II.I.K4	Interphone and intercom systems.
AM.II.I.K5	Very high frequency (VHF), high frequency (HF), and SATCOM systems.
AM.II.I.K6	Aircraft Communication Addressing and Reporting System (ACARS) theory, components, and operation.
AM.II.I.K7	Emergency locator transmitter (ELT).
AM.II.I.K8	Automatic direction finder (ADF).
AM.II.I.K9	VHF omnidirectional range (VOR) theory, components, and operation.
AM.II.I.K10	Distance measuring equipment (DME) theory, components, and operation.
AM.II.I.K11	Instrument landing system (ILS) theory, components, and operation.
AM.II.I.K12	Global positioning system (GPS) theory, components, and operation.
AM.II.I.K13	Traffic collision avoidance system (TCAS), theory, components, and operation.
AM.II.I.K14	Weather radar.
AM.II.I.K15	Ground proximity warning system (GPWS) theory, components, and operation.
AM.II.I.K16	Autopilot theory, components, and operation.
AM.II.I.K17	Auto-throttle theory, components, and operation.
AM.II.I.K18	Stability augmentation systems (SAS) (Rotorcraft).
AM.II.I.K19	Radio altimeter (RA) theory, components, and operation.
AM.II.I.K20	Automatic Dependent Surveillance-Broadcast (ADS-B) theory, components, and operation.
AM.II.I.K21	Transponder/encoder system.
Risk Management	*The applicant demonstrates the ability to identify, assess, and mitigate risks associated with:*
AM.II.I.R1	ELT testing procedures.
AM.II.I.R2	Performing maintenance on high power/high frequency systems (e.g., weather radar and SATCOM).
AM.II.I.R3	Wire harness routing.
AM.II.I.R4	Mounting antennas.
AM.II.I.R5	Electro-static discharge.
AM.II.I.R6	Working around live electrical systems.
Skills	*The applicant demonstrates the ability to:*
AM.II.I.S1	Make a list of required placards for communication and navigation avionic equipment.
AM.II.I.S2	Locate and explain autopilot inspection procedures.
AM.II.I.S3	List autopilot major components.

AM.II.I.S4	Locate and identify navigation and communication antennas.
AM.II.I.S5	Check VHF communications for operation.
AM.II.I.S6	Inspect a coaxial cable installation for security.
AM.II.I.S7	Check an emergency locator transmitter for operation.
AM.II.I.S8	Inspect ELT batteries for expiration date and locate proper testing procedures.
AM.II.I.S9	Inspect electronic equipment mounting base for security and condition.
AM.II.I.S10	Inspect electronic equipment shock mount bonding jumpers for resistance.
AM.II.I.S11	Inspect static discharge wicks for security and resistance.
AM.II.I.S12	Inspect a radio installation for security.
AM.II.I.S13	Locate and explain the installation procedures for antennas, including mounting and coaxial connections.

II. Airframe

Subject J. Aircraft Fuel Systems

Objective		*The following knowledge, risk management, and skill elements are required for aircraft fuel systems.*
Knowledge		*The applicant demonstrates understanding of:*
	AM.II.J.K1	Fuel system types.
	AM.II.J.K2	Fuel system components, including filters and selector valves.
	AM.II.J.K3	Aircraft fuel tanks/cells
	AM.II.J.K4	Fuel flow.
	AM.II.J.K5	Fuel transfer, fueling, and defueling.
	AM.II.J.K6	Fuel jettisoning/dump systems.
	AM.II.J.K7	Characteristics of fuel types.
	AM.II.J.K8	Fuel system maintenance and inspection.
	AM.II.J.K9	Fuel quantity indication.
Risk Management		*The applicant demonstrates the ability to identify, assess, and mitigate risks associated with:*
	AM.II.J.R1	Fuel system maintenance.
	AM.II.J.R2	Fuel system contamination.
	AM.II.J.R3	Fuel spills.
	AM.II.J.R4	Fuel system maintenance requiring fuel tank entry.
	AM.II.J.R5	Defueling aircraft.
Skills		*The applicant demonstrates the ability to:*
	AM.II.J.S1	Inspect, check, troubleshoot, or repair a fuel system.
	AM.II.J.S2	Inspect a metal, bladder, or integral fuel tank.
	AM.II.J.S3	Troubleshoot and repair aircraft fuel system.
	AM.II.J.S4	Inspect a fuel selector valve.
	AM.II.J.S5	Inspect and check manually-operated fuel valves for proper operation and leaks.
	AM.II.J.S6	Troubleshoot a fuel valve problem.
	AM.II.J.S7	Drain fuel system sump(s).
	AM.II.J.S8	Service a fuel system strainer.
	AM.II.J.S9	Inspect a fuel quantity indicating system.
	AM.II.J.S10	Locate fuel system operating instructions.
	AM.II.J.S11	Locate fuel system inspection procedures.
	AM.II.J.S12	Locate fuel system crossfeed procedures.
	AM.II.J.S13	Locate fuel system required placards.
	AM.II.J.S14	Locate fuel system defueling procedures.
	AM.II.J.S15	Troubleshoot fuel pressure warning system.
	AM.II.J.S16	Locate troubleshooting procedures for fuel temperature systems.
	AM.II.J.S17	Remove and install a fuel quantity transmitter.

II. Airframe

Subject K. Aircraft Electrical Systems

Objective
The following knowledge, risk management, and skill elements are required for aircraft electrical systems.

Knowledge
The applicant demonstrates understanding of:

AM.II.K.K1	Generators, DC generation systems, and DC power distribution systems.
AM.II.K.K2	Alternators, AC generation systems, and AC power distribution systems.
AM.II.K.K3	Starter generators.
AM.II.K.K4	constant speed drive (CSD) and integrated drive generator (IDG) systems and components.
AM.II.K.K5	Voltage regulators and over-volt and overcurrent protection.
AM.II.K.K6	Inverter systems.
AM.II.K.K7	Aircraft wiring sizes, types, selection, installation and circuit protection devices.
AM.II.K.K8	Derating factors in switch selection.
AM.II.K.K9	Aircraft wiring shielding.
AM.II.K.K10	Aircraft lightning protection.
AM.II.K.K11	Instrument or instrument panel removal and installation.
AM.II.K.K12	Aircraft lighting systems.
AM.II.K.K13	Electrical system troubleshooting.
AM.II.K.K14	Soldering preparation, types of solder, and flux usage.
AM.II.K.K15	Aircraft electrical connectors, splices, terminals, and switches.
AM.II.K.K16	Electrical system measurement, adjustment, and testing.
AM.II.K.K17	Aircraft battery troubleshooting and maintenance.

Risk Management
The applicant demonstrates the ability to identify, assess, and mitigate risks associated with:

AM.II.K.R1	Testing/troubleshooting electrical systems or components.
AM.II.K.R2	Connecting or disconnecting external power.
AM.II.K.R3	Maintenance on energized circuits/systems.
AM.II.K.R4	Maintenance in areas containing aircraft wiring.
AM.II.K.R5	Routing and securing wires and wire bundles.
AM.II.K.R6	Selecting the size of wire in an electrical circuit.
AM.II.K.R7	Selection or installation of wire terminals.
AM.II.K.R8	Effects of soldering.
AM.II.K.R9	Soldering practices.

Skills
The applicant demonstrates the ability to:

AM.II.K.S1	Inspect aircraft wiring to verify installation and routing.
AM.II.K.S2	Perform wire terminating and splicing.
AM.II.K.S3	Assemble an aircraft electrical connector.
AM.II.K.S4	Use a wiring circuit diagram to identify components.
AM.II.K.S5	Solder aircraft wiring.

AM.II.K.S6	Troubleshoot an airframe electrical circuit.
AM.II.K.S7	Install airframe electrical wiring, switches, or protective devices.
AM.II.K.S8	Secure wire bundles.
AM.II.K.S9	Determine an electrical load in a given aircraft system.
AM.II.K.S10	Install bonding jumpers.
AM.II.K.S11	Check output voltage of a DC generator.
AM.II.K.S12	Check the resistance of an electrical system component.
AM.II.K.S13	Inspect generator brush serviceability and brush spring tension.
AM.II.K.S14	Inspect and check anti-collision, position, and landing lights for proper operation.
AM.II.K.S15	Inspect components in an electrical system.
AM.II.K.S16	Troubleshoot a DC electrical system supplied by an AC electrical system.
AM.II.K.S17	Identify components in an electrical schematic where AC is rectified to a DC voltage.
AM.II.K.S18	Perform a continuity test to verify the condition of a conductor.
AM.II.K.S19	Perform a test on a conductor for a short to ground.
AM.II.K.S20	Perform a test on a conductor for a short to other conductors.

II. Airframe

Subject L. Ice and Rain Control Systems

Objective	*The following knowledge, risk management, and skill elements are required for aircraft ice and rain control systems.*
Knowledge	*The applicant demonstrates understanding of:*
AM.II.L.K1	Aircraft icing causes/effects.
AM.II.L.K2	Ice detection systems.
AM.II.L.K3	Aircraft and powerplant anti-ice systems and components.
AM.II.L.K4	De-ice systems and components.
AM.II.L.K5	Wiper blade, chemical, and pneumatic bleed air rain control systems.
AM.II.L.K6	Anti-icing and de-icing system maintenance.
AM.II.L.K7	Environmental conditions that degrade vision.
Risk Management	*The applicant demonstrates the ability to identify, assess, and mitigate risks associated with:*
AM.II.L.R1	System testing or maintenance.
AM.II.L.R2	Storage and handling of deicing fluids.
AM.II.L.R3	Selection and use of cleaning materials for heated windshields.
Skills	*The applicant demonstrates the ability to:*
AM.II.L.S1	Inspect and operationally check pitot-static anti-ice system.
AM.II.L.S2	Inspect and operationally check deicer boot.
AM.II.L.S3	Clean a pneumatic deicer boot.
AM.II.L.S4	Troubleshoot an electrically-heated pitot system.
AM.II.L.S5	Inspect thermal anti-ice systems.
AM.II.L.S6	Inspect and operationally check an electrically-heated windshield.
AM.II.L.S7	Locate and explain the procedures for inspecting an electrically-operated windshield wiper system.
AM.II.L.S8	Locate and explain the procedures for replacing blades on a windshield wiper system.
AM.II.L.S9	Locate and explain the procedures for inspecting a pneumatic rain removal system.

II. Airframe

Subject M. Airframe Fire Protection Systems

Objective	*The following knowledge, risk management, and skill elements are required for airframe fire protection systems.*
Knowledge	*The applicant demonstrates understanding of:*
AM.II.M.K1	Types of fires and aircraft fire zones.
AM.II.M.K2	Overheat and fire detection and warning systems.
AM.II.M.K3	Overheat and fire detection system maintenance and inspection.
AM.II.M.K4	Smoke and carbon monoxide detection systems.
AM.II.M.K5	Fire extinguishing agents.
AM.II.M.K6	Types of fire extinguishing systems.
AM.II.M.K7	Fire extinguishing system maintenance and inspection requirements.
Risk Management	*The applicant demonstrates the ability to identify, assess, and mitigate risks associated with:*
AM.II.M.R1	Maintenance on circuits associated with fire bottle squibs.
AM.II.M.R2	Use of PPEs when working on or testing fire extinguishing systems.
AM.II.M.R3	Fire extinguishing agents.
Skills	*The applicant demonstrates the ability to:*
AM.II.M.S1	Troubleshoot an aircraft fire detection or extinguishing system.
AM.II.M.S2	Determine proper container pressure for an installed fire extinguisher system.
AM.II.M.S3	Identify maintenance procedures for fire detection and extinguishing system(s) and system component(s).
AM.II.M.S4	Inspect a smoke and toxic gas detection system.
AM.II.M.S5	Inspect a carbon monoxide detector.
AM.II.M.S6	Locate and explain the procedures for checking a smoke detection system.
AM.II.M.S7	Locate and explain the procedures for inspecting an overheat detection system.
AM.II.M.S8	Inspect fire protection system cylinders and check for hydrostatic test date.
AM.II.M.S9	Inspect fire detection/protection system.
AM.II.M.S10	Perform operational check of fire detection/protection system.
AM.II.M.S11	Inspect fire extinguishing agent bottle discharge cartridge.
AM.II.M.S12	Inspect a continuous-loop type fire detection system.

II. Airframe

Subject N. Rotorcraft Fundamentals

Objective	*The following knowledge, risk management, and skill elements are required for rotorcraft fundamentals.*
Knowledge	*The applicant demonstrates understanding of:*
AM.II.N.K1	Rotorcraft aerodynamics.
AM.II.N.K2	Flight controls.
AM.II.N.K3	Transmissions.
AM.II.N.K4	Rigging requirements for rotary wing aircraft.
AM.II.N.K5	Design, type, and operation of rotor systems.
AM.II.N.K6	Helicopter skid shoe and tube inspection.
AM.II.N.K7	Rotor blade functions and construction.
AM.II.N.K8	Rotor vibrations, track, and balance.
AM.II.N.K9	Drive system vibrations and inspection.
Risk Management	*The applicant demonstrates the ability to identify, assess, and mitigate risks associated with:*
AM.II.N.R1	Working around helicopter blades during ground operations.
AM.II.N.R2	Ground-handling procedures.
AM.II.N.R3	Ground operations and functional tests.
AM.II.N.R4	Maintenance and inspection of rotorcraft systems and components.
Skills	*The applicant demonstrates the ability to:*
AM.II.N.S1	Locate components of a helicopter rotor system.
AM.II.N.S2	Locate helicopter rotor blade track and balance procedures.
AM.II.N.S3	Locate and explain procedures needed to rig helicopter controls.
AM.II.N.S4	Locate and explain procedures to track and balance a rotor system.

II. Airframe

Subject O. Water and Waste Systems

Objective	*The following knowledge, risk management, and skill elements are required for water and waste systems.*
Knowledge	*The applicant demonstrates understanding of:*
AM.II.O.K1	Potable water system components and operation.
AM.II.O.K2	Lavatory waste system components and operation.
AM.II.O.K3	Inspection and servicing requirements for water and waste systems.
Risk Management	*The applicant demonstrates the ability to identify, assess, and mitigate risks associated with:*
AM.II.O.R1	Servicing lavatory waste systems, including use of safety equipment.
Skills	*The applicant demonstrates the ability to:*
AM.II.O.S1	Locate and explain the procedures for servicing a lavatory waste system.
AM.II.O.S2	Locate and explain the procedures for servicing a potable water system.

III. Powerplant

Subject A. Reciprocating Engines

Objective	The following knowledge, risk management, and skill elements are required for aircraft reciprocating engines.
Knowledge	The applicant demonstrates understanding of:
AM.III.A.K1	Types of reciprocating engines.
AM.III.A.K2	Reciprocating engine operating principles/theory of operation.
AM.III.A.K3	Internal combustion engine operating principles/theory of operation.
AM.III.A.K4	Horizontally-opposed engine construction and internal components.
AM.III.A.K5	Radial engine construction and internal components.
AM.III.A.K6	Storage and preservation.
AM.III.A.K7	Reciprocating engine performance (e.g., PLANK, SFC).
AM.III.A.K8	Reciprocating engine maintenance and inspection.
AM.III.A.K9	Reciprocating engine ground operations.
AM.III.A.K10	Diesel engine operating principles/theory of operation.
Risk Management	The applicant demonstrates the ability to identify, assess, and mitigate risks associated with:
AM.III.A.R1	Maintenance that requires moving the propeller.
AM.III.A.R2	Preparation for and ground operation of a reciprocating engine.
AM.III.A.R3	Actions in the event of a reciprocating engine fire.
AM.III.A.R4	Use of other than manufacturer's procedures during maintenance.
Skills	The applicant demonstrates the ability to:
AM.III.A.S1	Perform a cylinder assembly inspection.
AM.III.A.S2	Operate and troubleshoot a reciprocating engine.
AM.III.A.S3	Install piston and knuckle/wrist pin(s).
AM.III.A.S4	Identify the parts of a cylinder.
AM.III.A.S5	Identify the parts of a crankshaft.
AM.III.A.S6	Identify and inspect various types of bearings.
AM.III.A.S7	Inspect and rig cable and push-pull engine controls.
AM.III.A.S8	Locate top dead-center position of number one cylinder.
AM.III.A.S9	Install a cylinder on a horizontally-opposed engine.

III. Powerplant

Subject B. Turbine Engines

Objective		The following knowledge, risk management, and skill elements are required for aircraft turbine engines.
Knowledge		The applicant demonstrates understanding of:
	AM.III.B.K1	Turbine engine operating principles/theory of operation.
	AM.III.B.K2	Types of turbine engines.
	AM.III.B.K3	Turbine engine construction and internal components.
	AM.III.B.K4	Turbine engine performance and monitoring.
	AM.III.B.K5	Turbine engine troubleshooting, maintenance, and inspection procedures.
	AM.III.B.K6	Procedures required after the installation of a turbine engine.
	AM.III.B.K7	Causes for turbine engine performance loss.
	AM.III.B.K8	Bleed air systems.
	AM.III.B.K9	Storage and preservation.
	AM.III.B.K10	Auxiliary power unit(s).
	AM.III.B.K11	Turbine engine adjustment and testing.
Risk Management		The applicant demonstrates the ability to identify, assess, and mitigate risks associated with:
	AM.III.B.R1	Operation of a turbine engine.
	AM.III.B.R2	Performing maintenance on a turbine engine.
	AM.III.B.R3	Actions in the event of a turbine engine fire.
	AM.III.B.R4	Foreign object damage.
Skills		The applicant demonstrates the ability to:
	AM.III.B.S1	Identify different turbine compressors.
	AM.III.B.S2	Identify different types of turbine engine blades.
	AM.III.B.S3	Identify components of turbine engines.
	AM.III.B.S4	Map airflow direction and pressure changes in turbine engines.
	AM.III.B.S5	Remove and install a fuel nozzle in a turbine engine.
	AM.III.B.S6	Inspect a combustion liner.
	AM.III.B.S7	Locate the procedures for the adjustment of a fuel control unit.
	AM.III.B.S8	Perform turbine engine inlet guide vane and compressor blade inspection.
	AM.III.B.S9	Locate the installation or removal procedures for a turbine engine.
	AM.III.B.S10	Locate and explain the procedure for trimming a turbine engine.
	AM.III.B.S11	Identify damaged turbine engine blades.
	AM.III.B.S12	Identify causes for turbine engine performance loss.
	AM.III.B.S13	Inspect the first two stages of a turbine fan or compressor for foreign object damage.

III. Powerplant

Subject C. Engine Inspection

Objective		*The following knowledge, risk management, and skill elements are required for aircraft engine inspections.*
Knowledge		*The applicant demonstrates understanding of:*
	AM.III.C.K1	Inspection requirements under 14 CFR part 43 and 14 CFR part 91.
	AM.III.C.K2	Identification of life-limited parts and their replacement interval.
	AM.III.C.K3	Special inspections.
	AM.III.C.K4	Use of FAA-approved data.
	AM.III.C.K5	Compliance with service letters, service bulletins, instructions for continued airworthiness, ADs, or TCDSs.
	AM.III.C.K6	Maintenance recordkeeping requirements under 14 CFR part 43.
	AM.III.C.K7	Engine component inspection, checking, and servicing.
	AM.III.C.K8	Engine mounts, mounting hardware, and the inspection and checking of each.
Risk Management		*The applicant demonstrates the ability to identify, assess, and mitigate risks associated with:*
	AM.III.C.R1	A compression test on a reciprocating engine.
	AM.III.C.R2	Maintenance on an operating reciprocating engine.
	AM.III.C.R3	Maintenance on an operating turbine engine.
Skills		*The applicant demonstrates the ability to:*
	AM.III.C.S1	Perform a compression check on a cylinder.
	AM.III.C.S2	Evaluate powerplant for compliance with FAA-approved or manufacturer data.
	AM.III.C.S3	Perform a powerplant records inspection.
	AM.III.C.S4	Inspect for compliance with applicable ADs.
	AM.III.C.S5	Determine engine installation eligibility.
	AM.III.C.S6	Determine compliance with engine specifications, TCDS, or engine listings.
	AM.III.C.S7	Perform a portion of a required inspection on an engine.
	AM.III.C.S8	Check engine controls for proper operation and adjustment.
	AM.III.C.S9	Inspect an engine for leaks after performing maintenance.
	AM.III.C.S10	Inspect an aircraft engine accessory for serviceability.
	AM.III.C.S11	Inspect engine records for time or cycles on life-limited parts.
	AM.III.C.S12	Perform an engine start and inspect engine operational parameters.
	AM.III.C.S13	Perform a portion of a 100-hour inspection on an engine in accordance with part 43.
	AM.III.C.S14	Inspect an engine mount to determine serviceability.

III. Powerplant

Subject D. Engine Instrument Systems

Objective	The following knowledge, risk management, and skill elements are required for aircraft engine instrument systems.
Knowledge	The applicant demonstrates understanding of:
AM.III.D.K1	Fuel flow.
AM.III.D.K2	Temperature (e.g., exhaust gas, oil, oil cylinder head, turbine inlet).
AM.III.D.K3	Engine speed indicating systems.
AM.III.D.K4	Pressure (e.g., air, fuel, manifold, oil).
AM.III.D.K5	Annunciator indicating systems (e.g., warning, caution, and advisory lights).
AM.III.D.K6	Torquemeters.
AM.III.D.K7	Engine pressure ratio (EPR).
AM.III.D.K8	Engine indicating and crew alerting system (EICAS).
AM.III.D.K9	Digital engine control module (e.g., full authority digital engine controls (FADEC)).
AM.III.D.K10	Electronic centralized aircraft monitor (ECAM).
AM.III.D.K11	Engine instrument range markings and instrument conditions.
Risk Management	The applicant demonstrates the ability to identify, assess, and mitigate risks associated with:
AM.III.D.R1	Maintenance damage to the instrument or indicating system.
AM.III.D.R2	Engine instrument calibration or instrument error.
Skills	The applicant demonstrates the ability to:
AM.III.D.S1	Troubleshoot an engine oil temperature/pressure instrument system.
AM.III.D.S2	Troubleshoot a low fuel pressure indicating system.
AM.III.D.S3	Remove, inspect, and install a fuel-flow transmitter.
AM.III.D.S4	Remove, inspect, and install fuel-flow gauge.
AM.III.D.S5	Identify components of an electric tachometer system.
AM.III.D.S6	Check fuel-flow transmitter power supply.
AM.III.D.S7	Inspect tachometer markings for accuracy.
AM.III.D.S8	Perform resistance measurements of thermocouple indication system.
AM.III.D.S9	Remove, inspect, and install turbine engine exhaust gas temperature (EGT) component.
AM.III.D.S10	Locate procedures for troubleshooting a turbine EPR system.
AM.III.D.S11	Troubleshoot a tachometer system.
AM.III.D.S12	Replace a cylinder head temperature thermocouple.
AM.III.D.S13	Inspect EGT probes.
AM.III.D.S14	Locate and inspect engine low fuel pressure warning system components.
AM.III.D.S15	Check aircraft engine manifold pressure gauge for proper operation.
AM.III.D.S16	Inspect a manifold pressure system.
AM.III.D.S17	Repair a low oil pressure warning system.

| AM.III.D.S18 | Troubleshoot an EGT indicating system. |
| AM.III.D.S19 | Inspect an oil temperature probe. |

III. Powerplant

Subject E. Engine Fire Protection Systems

Objective   *The following knowledge, risk management, and skill elements are required for aircraft engine fire protection systems.*

Knowledge   *The applicant demonstrates understanding of:*

AM.III.E.K1	Types of fires and engine fire zones.
AM.III.E.K2	Fire detection warning system operation.
AM.III.E.K3	Fire detection system maintenance and inspection requirements.
AM.III.E.K4	Fire extinguishing agents, types of systems, and operation.
AM.III.E.K5	Fire extinguishing system maintenance and inspection.

Risk Management   *The applicant demonstrates the ability to identify, assess, and mitigate risks associated with:*

AM.III.E.R1	Container discharge cartridges.
AM.III.E.R2	Extinguishing agents.
AM.III.E.R3	Maintenance on circuits associated with electrically-activated container discharge cartridges (squibs).

Skills   *The applicant demonstrates the ability to:*

AM.III.E.S1	Troubleshoot and repair an engine fire detection system.
AM.III.E.S2	Identify fire detection sensing units.
AM.III.E.S3	Inspect fire detection continuous loop system.
AM.III.E.S4	Inspect fire detection thermal switch or thermocouple system.
AM.III.E.S5	Locate troubleshooting procedures for a fire detection system.
AM.III.E.S6	Inspect engine fire extinguisher system blowout plugs.
AM.III.E.S7	Inspect a turbine engine fire extinguisher container.
AM.III.E.S8	Inspect fire extinguisher discharge circuit.
AM.III.E.S9	Troubleshoot and repair a fire extinguishing system.
AM.III.E.S10	Inspect a fire extinguisher container discharge cartridge (squib).
AM.III.E.S11	Inspect fire extinguisher container and determine hydrostatic test requirements.
AM.III.E.S12	Inspect flame detectors for operation.
AM.III.E.S13	Check operation of fire warning press-to-test and troubleshoot faults.
AM.III.E.S14	Identify continuous-loop fire detection system components.

III. Powerplant

Subject F. Engine Electrical Systems

Objective — The following knowledge, risk management, and skill elements are required for aircraft engine electrical systems.

Knowledge — The applicant demonstrates understanding of:

AM.III.F.K1	Generators.
AM.III.F.K2	Alternators.
AM.III.F.K3	Starter generators.
AM.III.F.K4	Voltage regulators and overvoltage and overcurrent protection.
AM.III.F.K5	DC generation systems.
AM.III.F.K6	AC generation systems.
AM.III.F.K7	The procedure for locating the correct electrical cable/wire size needed to fabricate a cable/wire.
AM.III.F.K8	The purpose and procedure for paralleling a dual-generator electrical system.
AM.III.F.K9	CSD and IDG systems and components.
AM.III.F.K10	Engine electrical wiring, switches, and protective devices.

Risk Management — The applicant demonstrates the ability to identify, assess, and mitigate risks associated with:

AM.III.F.R1	Polarity when performing electrical system maintenance.
AM.III.F.R2	Actions in response to a warning or caution annunciator light.
AM.III.F.R3	Maintenance on energized aircraft circuits/systems.
AM.III.F.R4	Routing and security of wiring near flammable fluid lines.

Skills — The applicant demonstrates the ability to:

AM.III.F.S1	Inspect engine electrical wiring, switches, and protective devices.
AM.III.F.S2	Determine suitability of a replacement component by part number.
AM.III.F.S3	Replace an engine-driven generator or alternator.
AM.III.F.S4	Inspect an engine-driven generator or alternator in accordance with manufacturer's instructions.
AM.III.F.S5	Troubleshoot an aircraft electrical generating system.
AM.III.F.S6	Remove and install an engine direct-drive electric starter.
AM.III.F.S7	Troubleshoot a direct-drive electric starter system.
AM.III.F.S8	Inspect an electrical system cable.
AM.III.F.S9	Determine wire size for engine electrical system.
AM.III.F.S10	Repair a broken engine electrical system wire.
AM.III.F.S11	Replace a wire bundle lacing.
AM.III.F.S12	Troubleshoot an electrical system using a schematic or wiring diagram.
AM.III.F.S13	Fabricate a bonding jumper.
AM.III.F.S14	Inspect a turbine engine starter generator.
AM.III.F.S15	Inspect engine electrical connectors.

III. Powerplant

Subject G. Engine Lubrication Systems

Objective	*The following knowledge, risk management, and skill elements are required for aircraft engine lubrication systems.*
Knowledge	*The applicant demonstrates understanding of:*
AM.III.G.K1	Types, grades, and uses of engine oil.
AM.III.G.K2	Lubrication system operation and components.
AM.III.G.K3	Wet-sump system.
AM.III.G.K4	Dry-sump system.
AM.III.G.K5	Chip detectors.
AM.III.G.K6	Lubrication system maintenance, inspection, servicing, and analysis.
AM.III.G.K7	Excessive aircraft engine oil consumption.
Risk Management	*The applicant demonstrates the ability to identify, assess, and mitigate risks associated with:*
AM.III.G.R1	Use or mixing of engine oils.
AM.III.G.R2	Following other than manufacturer's recommendations regarding the use of engine lubricants.
AM.III.G.R3	Handling, storage, and disposal of used lubricating oil.
Skills	*The applicant demonstrates the ability to:*
AM.III.G.S1	Inspect an oil cooler or oil lines.
AM.III.G.S2	Determine the correct type of oil for a specific engine.
AM.III.G.S3	Identify turbine engine oil filter bypass indicator.
AM.III.G.S4	Determine approved oils for different climatic temperatures.
AM.III.G.S5	Locate procedures for obtaining oil samples.
AM.III.G.S6	Inspect an oil filter or screen.
AM.III.G.S7	Perform oil pressure adjustment.
AM.III.G.S8	Identify oil system components.
AM.III.G.S9	Replace an oil system component.
AM.III.G.S10	Identify oil system flow.
AM.III.G.S11	Troubleshoot an engine oil pressure malfunction.
AM.III.G.S12	Troubleshoot an engine oil temperature system.
AM.III.G.S13	Identify types of metal found in an oil filter.
AM.III.G.S14	Remove and inspect an engine chip detector.

III. Powerplant

Subject H. Ignition and Starting Systems

Objective	The following knowledge, risk management, and skill elements are required for aircraft ignition and starting systems.
Knowledge	The applicant demonstrates understanding of:
AM.III.H.K1	Ignition system theory.
AM.III.H.K2	Spark plug theory.
AM.III.H.K3	Shower of sparks and impulse coupling.
AM.III.H.K4	Three electrical circuits of a magneto system.
AM.III.H.K5	Solid-state ignition systems.
AM.III.H.K6	Digital engine control module (e.g., FADEC).
AM.III.H.K7	Engine starters.
AM.III.H.K8	Magneto system components and operation.
AM.III.H.K9	Turbine engine ignition systems.
Risk Management	The applicant demonstrates the ability to identify, assess, and mitigate risks associated with:
AM.III.H.R1	Advanced and retarded ignition timing (piston engine).
AM.III.H.R2	Maintenance on engines with capacitor discharge ignition systems.
AM.III.H.R3	Working around reciprocating engines with an ungrounded magneto.
Skills	The applicant demonstrates the ability to:
AM.III.H.S1	Set magneto internal timing.
AM.III.H.S2	Time magneto to engine.
AM.III.H.S3	Remove, clean, and install spark plug.
AM.III.H.S4	Troubleshoot and repair an ignition system.
AM.III.H.S5	Inspect an electrical starting system.
AM.III.H.S6	Inspect magneto breaker points.
AM.III.H.S7	Inspect an ignition harness.
AM.III.H.S8	Inspect a magneto impulse coupling.
AM.III.H.S9	Troubleshoot an electrical starting system.
AM.III.H.S10	Troubleshoot ignition switch circuit.
AM.III.H.S11	Inspect and check gap of spark plugs.
AM.III.H.S12	Identify the correct spark plugs used for replacement installation.
AM.III.H.S13	Troubleshoot a turbine or reciprocating engine ignition system.
AM.III.H.S14	Identify the correct igniter plug and replace turbine engine igniter plugs.
AM.III.H.S15	Troubleshoot turbine engine igniters.
AM.III.H.S16	Inspect turbine engine ignition system.
AM.III.H.S17	Inspect igniters.

III. Powerplant

Subject I. Engine Fuel and Fuel Metering Systems

Objective	The following knowledge, risk management, and skill elements are required for engine fuel and fuel metering systems.
Knowledge	The applicant demonstrates understanding of:
AM.III.I.K1	Fuel/air ratio and fuel metering, and carburetor theory and operation.
AM.III.I.K2	Float carburetor theory, components, operation, and adjustment.
AM.III.I.K3	Pressure carburetor theory, operation, and adjustment.
AM.III.I.K4	Continuous-flow fuel injection theory, components, operation, troubleshooting and adjustment.
AM.III.I.K5	Digital engine control module (e.g., FADEC).
AM.III.I.K6	Hydromechanical fuel control system design and components.
AM.III.I.K7	Fuel nozzles and manifolds design, operation, and maintenance.
AM.III.I.K8	Components, theory, and operation of turbine engine fuel metering system.
AM.III.I.K9	Inspection requirements for an engine fuel system.
AM.III.I.K10	Fuel system operation.
AM.III.I.K11	Fuel heaters.
AM.III.I.K12	Fuel lines.
AM.III.I.K13	Fuel pumps.
AM.III.I.K14	Fuel valves.
AM.III.I.K15	Fuel filters.
AM.III.I.K16	Engine fuel drains.
Risk Management	The applicant demonstrates the ability to identify, assess, and mitigate risks associated with:
AM.III.I.R1	Adjusting a turbine engine fuel control.
AM.III.I.R2	Adjusting reciprocating engine fuel control systems.
AM.III.I.R3	Handling of fuel metering system components that may contain fuel.
AM.III.I.R4	Considerations during fuel system maintenance.
AM.III.I.R5	Handling of engine fuel control units that may contain fuel.
Skills	The applicant demonstrates the ability to:
AM.III.I.S1	Inspect, troubleshoot, and repair a continuous-flow fuel injection system.
AM.III.I.S2	Remove, inspect, and install a turbine engine fuel nozzle.
AM.III.I.S3	Identify carburetor components.
AM.III.I.S4	Identify fuel and air flow through a float-type carburetor.
AM.III.I.S5	Remove and install a carburetor main metering jet.
AM.III.I.S6	Inspect a carburetor fuel inlet screen.
AM.III.I.S7	Adjust a continuous-flow fuel injection system.
AM.III.I.S8	Inspect the needle, seat, and float level on a float-type carburetor.
AM.III.I.S9	Remove and install a float-type carburetor.

AM.III.I.S10	Adjust carburetor idle speed and mixture.
AM.III.I.S11	Locate procedures for a turbine engine revolutions per minute (rpm) overspeed inspection.
AM.III.I.S12	Inspect fuel metering cockpit controls for proper adjustment.
AM.III.I.S13	Locate procedures for adjusting a hydromechanical fuel control unit.
AM.III.I.S14	Locate and explain procedures for removing and installing a turbine engine fuel control unit.
AM.III.I.S15	Identify components of an engine fuel system.
AM.III.I.S16	Remove and install an engine-driven fuel pump.
AM.III.I.S17	Inspect a remotely-operated fuel valve for proper operation.
AM.III.I.S18	Locate and identify fuel selector placards.
AM.III.I.S19	Inspect a main fuel filter assembly for leaks.
AM.III.I.S20	Inspect fuel boost pump.
AM.III.I.S21	Locate and identify a turbine engine fuel heater.
AM.III.I.S22	Inspect fuel pressure warning light function.
AM.III.I.S23	Adjust fuel pump fuel pressure.
AM.III.I.S24	Inspect engine fuel system fluid lines and components.
AM.III.I.S25	Troubleshoot abnormal fuel pressure.
AM.III.I.S26	Locate the procedures for troubleshooting a turbine engine fuel heater system.
AM.III.I.S27	Remove, clean, and reinstall an engine fuel filter.
AM.III.I.S28	Troubleshoot engine fuel pressure fluctuation.
AM.III.I.S29	Inspect fuel selector valve.
AM.III.I.S30	Determine correct fuel nozzle spray pattern.

Subject J. Reciprocating Engine Induction and Cooling Systems

Objective	The following knowledge, risk management, and skill elements are required for aircraft reciprocating engine induction and cooling systems.
Knowledge	The applicant demonstrates understanding of:
AM.III.J.K1	Reciprocating engine induction and cooling system theory, components, and operation.
AM.III.J.K2	Causes and effects of induction system icing.
AM.III.J.K3	Superchargers and controls.
AM.III.J.K4	Turbochargers, intercoolers, and controls.
AM.III.J.K5	Augmenter cooling system.
AM.III.J.K6	Induction system filtering.
AM.III.J.K7	Carburetor heaters.
AM.III.J.K8	Pressure cowling air flow and control.
AM.III.J.K9	Reciprocating engine baffle and seal installation.
AM.III.J.K10	Liquid cooling system theory, components, and operation.
Risk Management	The applicant demonstrates the ability to identify, assess, and mitigate risks associated with:
AM.III.J.R1	Maintenance on turbochargers.
AM.III.J.R2	Ground operation of aircraft engines.
AM.III.J.R3	Maintenance-related FOD.
AM.III.J.R4	Chemicals used in liquid cooling systems.
Skills	The applicant demonstrates the ability to:
AM.III.J.S1	Inspect a carburetor heat system.
AM.III.J.S2	Inspect an alternate air valve for proper operation.
AM.III.J.S3	Inspect an induction system drain for proper operation.
AM.III.J.S4	Inspect engine exhaust augmenter cooling system.
AM.III.J.S5	Service an induction air filter.
AM.III.J.S6	Inspect a turbocharger for leaks and security.
AM.III.J.S7	Inspect and service a turbocharger waste gate.
AM.III.J.S8	Inspect an induction system for obstruction.
AM.III.J.S9	Inspect an air intake manifold for leaks.
AM.III.J.S10	Locate the proper specifications for coolant used in a liquid-cooled engine.
AM.III.J.S11	Inspect reciprocating engine cooling ducting (rigid or flexible) or baffle seals.
AM.III.J.S12	Identify components of a turbocharger induction system.
AM.III.J.S13	Identify exhaust augmenter-cooled engine components.
AM.III.J.S14	Inspect an air inlet duct for security.
AM.III.J.S15	Perform an induction and cooling system inspection.
AM.III.J.S16	Repair a cylinder baffle.

AM.III.J.S17   Inspect cylinder baffling.

AM.III.J.S18   Inspect cowl flap system for normal operation.

AM.III.J.S19   Inspect cylinder cooling fins.

III. Powerplant

Subject K. Turbine Engine Air Systems

Objective   The following knowledge, risk management, and skill elements are required for aircraft turbine engine air systems.

Knowledge   The applicant demonstrates understanding of:

AM.III.K.K1	Air cooling system theory, components, and operation.
AM.III.K.K2	Turbine engine cowling air flow.
AM.III.K.K3	Turbine engine internal cooling.
AM.III.K.K4	Turbine engine baffle and seal installation.
AM.III.K.K5	Turbine engine insulation blankets and shrouds.
AM.III.K.K6	Turbine engine induction system theory, components, and operation.
AM.III.K.K7	Turbine engine bleed air system theory, components, and operation.
AM.III.K.K8	Turbine engine anti-ice system

Risk Management   The applicant demonstrates the ability to identify, assess, and mitigate risks associated with:

AM.III.K.R1	Maintenance on compressor bleed air systems.
AM.III.K.R2	Ground operation of aircraft engines following other than manufacturer's instructions.

Skills   The applicant demonstrates the ability to:

AM.III.K.S1	Perform an induction and cooling system inspection.
AM.III.K.S2	Identify location of turbine engine insulation blankets.
AM.III.K.S3	Identify turbine engine cooling air flow.
AM.III.K.S4	Inspect turbine engine cooling ducting (rigid or flexible) or baffle seals.
AM.III.K.S5	Inspect a turbine engine air intake anti-ice system.
AM.III.K.S6	Identify turbine engine ice and rain protection system components.
AM.III.K.S7	Inspect a particle separator.
AM.III.K.S8	Inspect/check a bleed air system.

III. Powerplant

Subject L. Engine Exhaust and Reverser Systems

Objective	The following knowledge, risk management, and skill elements are required for aircraft engine exhaust and reverser systems.

Knowledge — *The applicant demonstrates understanding of:*

AM.III.L.K1	Reciprocating engine exhaust system theory, components, operation, and inspection.
AM.III.L.K2	Turbine engine exhaust system theory, components, operation, and inspection.
AM.III.L.K3	Noise suppression theory, components, and operation (e.g., mufflers, hush kits, augmenter tubes).
AM.III.L.K4	Thrust reverser theory, components, and operation.

Risk Management — *The applicant demonstrates the ability to identify, assess, and mitigate risks associated with:*

AM.III.L.R1	Maintenance and inspection of exhaust system components.
AM.III.L.R2	Operation of turbine engine reversing systems.
AM.III.L.R3	Operation of reciprocating engines with exhaust systems leaks.
AM.III.L.R4	Exhaust system failures.
AM.III.L.R5	Ground operation of aircraft engines.

Skills — *The applicant demonstrates the ability to:*

AM.III.L.S1	Identify the type of exhaust system on a particular aircraft.
AM.III.L.S2	Inspect a turbine engine exhaust system component.
AM.III.L.S3	Inspect a reciprocating engine exhaust system.
AM.III.L.S4	Inspect exhaust system internal baffles or diffusers.
AM.III.L.S5	Inspect exhaust heat exchanger.
AM.III.L.S6	Locate procedures for testing and troubleshooting a turbine thrust reverser system.
AM.III.L.S7	Perform a pressure leak check of a reciprocating engine exhaust system.

III. Powerplant

Subject M. Propellers

Objective	The following knowledge, risk management, and skill elements are required for aircraft propellers.
Knowledge	The applicant demonstrates understanding of:
AM.III.M.K1	Propeller theory and operation.
AM.III.M.K2	Types of propellers and blade design.
AM.III.M.K3	Pitch control and adjustment.
AM.III.M.K4	Constant speed propeller and governor theory and operation.
AM.III.M.K5	Turbine engine propeller reverse/beta range operation.
AM.III.M.K6	Propeller servicing, maintenance, and inspection requirements.
AM.III.M.K7	Procedures for removal and installation of a propeller.
AM.III.M.K8	Propeller TCDS.
AM.III.M.K9	Propeller synchronization systems.
AM.III.M.K10	Propeller ice control systems.
Risk Management	The applicant demonstrates the ability to identify, assess, and mitigate risks associated with:
AM.III.M.R1	Ground operation.
AM.III.M.R2	Propeller maintenance and inspections.
Skills	The applicant demonstrates the ability to:
AM.III.M.S1	Remove and install a propeller.
AM.III.M.S2	Check blade static tracking.
AM.III.M.S3	Inspect a propeller for condition and airworthiness.
AM.III.M.S4	Measure propeller blade angle.
AM.III.M.S5	Perform a minor repair to a metal propeller blade.
AM.III.M.S6	Perform propeller lubrication.
AM.III.M.S7	Locate and explain the procedures for balancing a fixed-pitch propeller.
AM.III.M.S8	Adjust a propeller governor.
AM.III.M.S9	Identify propeller range of operation.
AM.III.M.S10	Perform a 100-hour inspection of a propeller and determine airworthiness.
AM.III.M.S11	Determine what minor propeller alterations are acceptable using the propeller specifications, TCDS, and listings.
AM.III.M.S12	Inspect and repair a propeller anti-icing or de-icing system.

Appendix 1: Practical Test Roles, Responsibilities, and Outcomes

Applicant Responsibilities

The applicant is responsible for demonstrating acceptable knowledge of the established standards for knowledge, skill, and risk management elements in all subjects appropriate to the certificate and rating sought. The applicant should use this ACS and its references in preparation to take the oral and practical test.

An applicant is not permitted to know, before testing begins, which selections from each subject area are to be included in his/her test. Therefore, an applicant should be well prepared in all knowledge, risk management, and skill elements included in the ACS.

The oral portion of the test consists of questions specific to the topics associated with the codes on the Airman Knowledge Test Report (AKTR) as well as additional questions that are randomly selected by the Mechanic Test Generator (MTG). During the Oral portion of the test the applicant is **not** allowed to use any reference material to answer the oral questions asked by the examiner. Applicants will need to demonstrate acceptable knowledge of the subjects missed on the FAA knowledge test. The practical portion of the test continues with questioning, specific to the projects being tested.

The practical portion of the test continues with practical questioning, specific to the projects being tested. The applicant is allowed to use reference materials to answer the practical questions that are asked while the practical portion (projects) of the test is being administered.

The practical (skill) portion of the tests are significant as they measure the applicant's ability to logically think and objectively apply their knowledge, while demonstrating the physical skills that enable them to carry out aircraft maintenance in a safe manner. Satisfactory demonstration of each skill tested is evidence the applicant meets the acceptable degree of competency for the certificate or rating sought.

All applicants demonstrate an approval for return to service standard, where applicable, and demonstrate the ability to locate and apply the required reference materials. In instances where an approval for return to service standard cannot be achieved, the applicant explains why the return to service standard was not met (e.g., when tolerances are outside of a product's limitations).

Evaluator Responsibilities

The evaluator asks the applicant to provide the AKTRs prior to generating the test planning sheet. All deficient knowledge areas, as indicated by the ACS codes on the AKTRs, are retested during the oral portion of the test. If the applicant scores 100 percent on the knowledge exam, the minimum number of questions are asked during the oral portion of the test.

The evaluator generates a complete test planning sheet to conduct the oral and practical test. The evaluator includes all the questions and projects obtained from the internet-based Mechanic Test Generator (MTG) at https://avinfo.faa.gov/DsgReg/Login.aspx. The MTG includes oral questions from the knowledge elements of the ACS to retest those topics missed on the FAA knowledge exams, as well as a minimum number of additional oral questions, and these should be asked during the oral portion of the test.

The MTG includes questions on the knowledge and risk management elements of the ACS, specific to the selected projects; and these should be asked, in context, during the practical demonstration portion of the test. The applicant is allowed to use reference material for those questions that are given as part of the practical demonstration portion of the test. The evaluator personally observes all practical projects performed by the applicant. The practical portion of the test includes an ongoing evaluation of knowledge and risk management, while evaluating the skill. The evaluator who conducts the practical test is responsible for determining that the applicant meets acceptable standards of knowledge and skill in the assigned subject areas within the appropriate ACS.

The evaluator should be aware that any information on the test that is in parentheses ( ) is additional or clarifying information. It is not expected that the applicant will recite all the information in parentheses however, it is acceptable as an alternative to what is stated in the answer. The applicant is allowed to use reference material for those questions that are given as part of the practical demonstration portion of the test. For this reason it is imperative that the examiner ensure that the oral and practical portions of the tests are kept separate.

The following terms may be reviewed with the applicant prior to, or during, element assignment:

1. **Inspect** means to examine (with or without inspection enhancing tools/equipment).
2. **Check** means to verify proper operation.
3. **Troubleshoot** means to analyze and identify malfunctions.
4. **Service** means to perform functions that assure continued operation.
5. **Repair** means to correct a defective condition; and repair of an airframe or powerplant system includes component replacement and adjustment.
6. **Overhaul** means to disassemble, clean, inspect, repair as necessary, and reassemble.

In the integrated ACS framework, the sections contain subjects, which are further broken down into knowledge elements (i.e., K1), risk management elements (i.e., R1), and skill elements (i.e., S1). Knowledge and risk management elements are also evaluated during the knowledge testing phase of the airman certification process. The evaluator administering the oral and practical test must not combine subjects/elements during testing.

Further information regarding the requirements for conducting a practical test is contained in the current revision of FAA Order 8900.1 or FAA Order 8900.2, as applicable.

Made in the USA
Monee, IL
12 October 2023

44454206R00037